PLANET PROBLEM SOLVERS

TRASH FOR TREASURE

A Look at Sustainable Swaps

PAPER

PLASTIC

GLASS

by Heather DiLorenzo Williams

NorwoodHouse Press

Norwood House Press
For more information about Norwood House Press please visit our website at www.norwoodhousepress.com or call 866-565-2900.
© 2023 Norwood House Press.
All rights reserved. No part of this book may be reproduced or utilized in any form or by any means without written permission from the publisher.

Credits
Editor: Mari Bolte
Designer: Sara Radka

Photo Credits
Cover: ©Nomad / Getty images; page 1: ©Sergiy Trofimov Photography / Getty Images; page 3: ©David Sailors / Getty Images; page 3: ©Cavan Images / Getty Images; page 3: ©RUSS ROHDE / Getty Images; page 5: ©Carmen Martínez Torrón / Getty Images; page 6: ©Surasak Suwanmake / Getty Images; page 7: ©Stevica Mrdja / EyeEm / Getty Images; page 9: ©nashrambler / Getty Images; page 9: ©Sky and glass / Shutterstock; page 9: ©cgdeaw / Getty Images; page 10: ©JGI/Jamie Grill / Getty Images; page 12: ©Martin Poole / Getty Images; page 15: ©VisionsofAmerica/Joe Sohm / Getty Images; page 16: ©Makiko Tanigawa / Getty Images; page 17: ©Capelle.r / Getty Images; page 21: ©Jacobs Stock Photography Ltd / Getty Images; page 22: © / EPA.gov; page 23: ©Getty Images / Stringer / Getty Images; page 24: ©georgeclerk / Getty Images; page 25: ©David McNew / Staff / Getty Images; page 29: ©mark_vyz / Shutterstock; page 30: ©AUGIER/OCEAN CLEANUP/SIPA / Newscom; page 31: ©COVER Images/ZUMA Press / Newscom; page 32: ©Christopher Furlong / Staff / Getty Images; page 33: ©Andrew Sacks / Stringer / Getty Images; page 34: ©Neilson Barnard / Staff / Getty Images; page 35: ©KRISTOPHER SKINNER/KRTC / Newscom; page 37: ©David R. Frazier / DanitaDelimont.com / "Danita Delimont Photography" / Newscom; page 41: ©SolStock / Getty Images; page 42: ©Imgorthand / Getty Images(middle); page 45: ©SolStock / Getty Images

Library of Congress Cataloging-in-Publication Data
Library of Congress Cataloging-in-Publication Data has been filed and is available at catalog.loc.gov

Hardcover ISBN: 978-1-68450-781-8
Paperback ISBN: 978-1-68404-745-1

353N—082022
Manufactured in the United States of America in North Mankato, Minnesota.

TABLE OF CONTENTS

CHAPTER 1

TOSSED AWAY

In 2010, 16-year-old Boyan Slat was scuba diving in Greece. He was hoping to see underwater life up close. What he saw instead amazed him. Beneath the blue water of the Mediterranean Sea was a world of trash. Slat started doing research. He discovered that the world's oceans are filled with plastic. He also found that no one was really trying to solve this problem. The amount of garbage just kept growing. Slat knew the answer was out there. He made an invention. It could remove 90 percent of plastic from the world's oceans by 2040. But trash is more than just an ocean problem.

Humans create garbage. It's just a natural part of living. But the United States is the most wasteful country in the world. Four percent of the world's people live in the US. However, its citizens produce 12 percent of the world's trash. The average person in the US creates around 1,700 pounds (771 kilograms) of trash per year.

How many trash cans are in your house?
How many recycling bins?

Scientists estimate that there are more pieces of plastic in the ocean than stars in the galaxy!

Most of this trash ends up in landfills. These are large areas of land where trash is dumped. Many states say their landfills will be full in five to 20 years. Trash also ends up on streets and sidewalks. This waste washes into streams and rivers. Then, it flows into the ocean. Anywhere from 8 to 16.5 million tons (7.3 to 15 million metric tons) of trash wash into the world's oceans each year.

One of the biggest problems is plastic. Most of it comes from single-use items. These include baggies, disposable water bottles, straws, and grocery bags. Most people only use these items for a few minutes. But they take hundreds of years to **decompose** in a landfill. Americans send about 27 million tons (24.5 million metric tons) of plastic to landfills yearly.

More than 100,000 fish, turtles, and other marine animals die as a result of plastic pollution every year.

More Plastic than Fish

Boyan Slat was just 16 when he claimed that he saw more plastic than fish under the ocean's waves. Back in 2010, Slat's observation may have been an exaggeration. But it could also be the future. If nothing is done to clean up the seas, scientists estimate the ocean will actually contain more plastic than fish by 2050. Sea creatures cannot tell the difference between plastic and a good meal. Rescued injured sea turtles often have bellies full of plastic. Fish eat plastic too. And then, humans eat the fish—and the plastic. The ocean is simply no place for plastic.

Dead or injured wildlife often have tiny pieces of microplastic inside their bodies.

Eighty percent of the trash in the ocean is plastic. Plastic can hurt fish and other sea life. They get tangled in bags and can holders. Animals get injured or can even drown. Over time, plastic in the ocean breaks down into tiny pieces of microplastics. Animals think it is food. But they cannot digest the plastic bits. Chemicals in plastic also **leach** into the water. The water becomes **contaminated**.

Chemicals from plastic also leach into soil. Water in soil absorbs the chemicals. These chemicals eventually end up in the water supply. People and animals who use that water are at risk.

Most plastic is recyclable. That means it can be turned into something else. But less than one-tenth actually makes it to recycling centers. The rest is thrown away. Most of it is incinerated at landfills. This means it is burned.

Burning plastic produces harmful substances called toxins. Toxins **pollute** the air. That's the same air we breathe. You may think of coal-fired power plants when you think of air pollution. But burning trash produces more! Burning plastic puts out **carbon monoxide**, mercury, and lead. These toxins cause breathing problems and other health issues. They also harm Earth's atmosphere.

Some trash incinerators are filtered. This helps keep toxins from entering the air. But the toxins from filtered systems end up in other places. Some of what is filtered is washed away. It enters the local water system. Some turns to ash and falls on the ground. It gets into the soil and eventually the water. Ash also blows away and clogs up the air.

Every 15.5 hours, people in the US throw out enough plastic to fill the Dallas Cowboys' AT&T Stadium, the largest NFL stadium in the country, which can hold as many as 100,000 spectators!

Aluminum and other metals can be recycled and made into new cans and other items.

Plastic makes up most of America's trash. But people throw away many other items. A lot of this happens because of planned **obsolescence**. This means that things are made to be thrown away after a certain amount of time. Items like straws and food containers are meant to be used once. Others break or wear out over time. Coffee makers, phones, and even cars stop working eventually. Repairs often cost more than buying a replacement. The old items end up in junkyards and landfills. But many can be recycled.

Americans throw away 11 million tons (10 million metric tons) of glass each year. Glass is completely recyclable. It can be made into new glass. Glass does not produce harmful chemicals when it breaks down. It can be recycled again and again. But only around one-third actually makes it to recycling centers. The rest ends up in landfills. Glass can take 1 to 2 million years to decompose. It just takes up space.

Metal is another common waste item. Like glass, it can be recycled many times. Soda cans, food cans, and baking foil are some examples. Even the foil tops of yogurt containers and empty hairspray cans can be recycled.

Take a look around your family's kitchen. What do you see that can be recycled that often gets thrown out with the trash?

Another thing taking up landfill space is paper. Americans throw away about 1 billion trees' worth of paper each year. Between 16 and 25 percent of landfill space is paper. Magazines, newspapers, paper plates, and cups are some of those items. But most is paper from offices and schools. A single family throws away 13,000 individual sheets every year.

There is good news, though. Paper is also the most-recycled form of waste. Americans recycle around 68 percent of paper. This includes newspapers and boxes. Recycling paper instead of throwing it away saves new trees from being cut down. It also reduces landfill space. And it saves energy.

But not every piece of paper can be recycled. Many greeting cards are sent during the winter holidays. People in the US mail around 1.3 billion holiday cards each December. Many greeting cards can be recycled. But anything with "extras" cannot. Glossy ink, glitter, ribbons, and added photos turn cards into trash.

One ton (0.9 metric tons) of recycled paper can save 17 trees.

Americans also throw away food, yard waste, rubber, wood, and fabric. Food and yard waste take up more landfill space than almost any other item. Food might not sound too bad. But food waste creates greenhouse gases. These gases damage Earth's atmosphere.

What do you do with old clothes, towels, or blankets? Chances are, they're in a landfill now. Most of the rubber waste in landfills is old tires and shoes. People also throw away wooden furniture, crates, and pallets. Broken electronics often end up in landfills too. Many of these items can be recycled, repurposed, or reused.

Recycling takes effort. Some people are willing to make new things from the old. But others just want the next new thing. It's easier to just throw the old thing away.

All that trash piles up. There is a **garbage patch** in the Pacific Ocean large enough to hold the state of Texas—twice. And if we stacked the holiday cards sold each year in the US, they would fill a football field 10 stories high. But if we all work together and make a few changes, we can make a big difference.

Where in your neighborhood can you take old cell phones and other items like furniture and appliances for recycling?

Americans throw away more than 12 million tons (10.9 metric tons) of old furniture each year. Not all of it makes it to a landfill.

CHAPTER 2

OLD INTO NEW

Recycling is one of the easiest ways to reduce waste. To recycle an item means to turn it into reusable material. About 75 percent of the 200 million tons (181.4 million metric tons) of garbage Americans make could be recycled in some way.

Before it is taken to a recycling facility, plastic must be sorted and cleaned.

Composting food and yard waste creates a nutrient-rich substance called humus that can be used as fertilizer.

Turning old into new uses less energy than starting fresh. Most paper can become new paper. All glass can be recycled to make new glass. Metal can be melted down and reshaped. It can even be made into new, different things. And your leftovers from last night can be recycled. Food is recycled by **composting**.

The amount of waste recycled in the US has gone up over the past 50 years. In the 1970s, many cities began looking for solutions to their waste problems. People also got interested in cleaning the air and water. Earth Day was created. The Environmental Protection Agency (EPA) was founded. Cities added recycling programs to their weekly trash pickup.

If people in the US recycled 75 percent of their waste, 1.1 million new jobs in manufacturing, recycling, and garbage processing would be created by the year 2030.

Recycling programs have many benefits. They do more than keep trash out of landfills. Recycling helps the environment. Keeping plastics out of landfills and incinerators keeps toxins out of the air and water supply. Careful recycling also means fewer waste items end up in streams, rivers, and the ocean. Recycling 75 percent of waste would greatly reduce pollution by the year 2030.

Recycling programs also help communities. They create jobs. Everyone in the community benefits. Recycling programs lead to nine times more jobs than landfills and trash incinerators. There are so many items that can be recycled or reused in different ways. This means there are more, different jobs out there. Recycling centers, companies that make new materials, and even thrift stores are some of the places people can work.

Traditional recycling is big business. Items must be collected. This is usually part of a community trash pickup. Pickups are either single-stream or multi-stream. Single-stream means all items are placed in one container. They are then sorted and cleaned. In a multi-stream program, people sort their items first. These programs create thousands of jobs.

How many recycling bins would you need to create a multi-stream recycling system in your house?

Today, most cities in America have recycling programs. Recycling collection and community drop-off points make the process easier than ever. Still, not everyone recycles. And some do not always do it the right way.

Sorting items correctly is important. If nonrecyclable items are mixed with recyclable ones, the whole batch could end up in the landfill anyway. People accidentally mix in items that can't be recycled. One example is paper coffee cups. These cups have a thin plastic lining that must be separated from the paper.

Dirty items don't belong, either. As many as one out of every four items in a recycling bin are either dirty or nonrecyclable. If there are not enough workers to sort or clean the items, they are sent to the trash.

Taking a few minutes to wash items before putting them in the recycling bin can help keep this from happening. Careful label-reading is also important. Plastics that can be recycled are called thermoplastics. They are labeled with the recycle symbol.

Look at the recycling logos on page 38. Which are you familiar with?

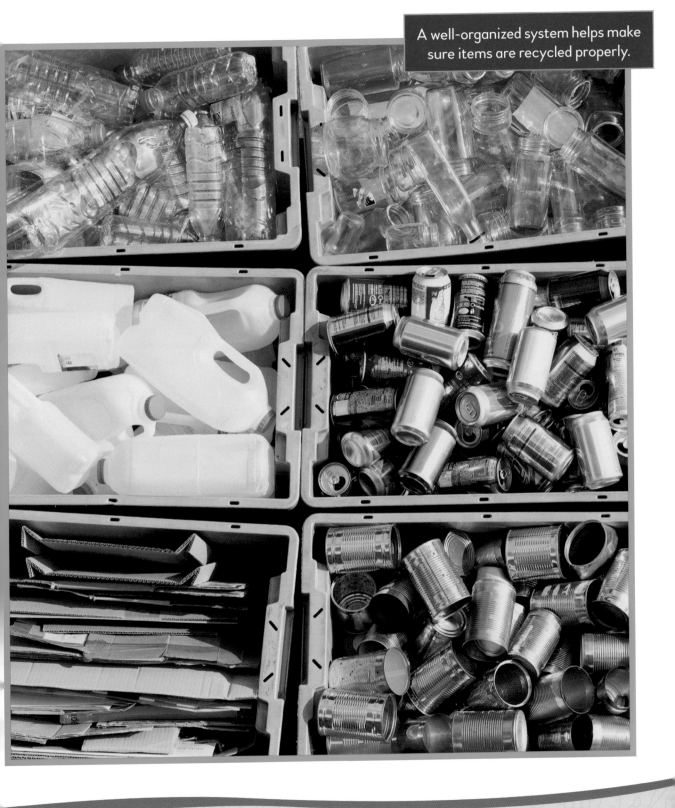

A well-organized system helps make sure items are recycled properly.

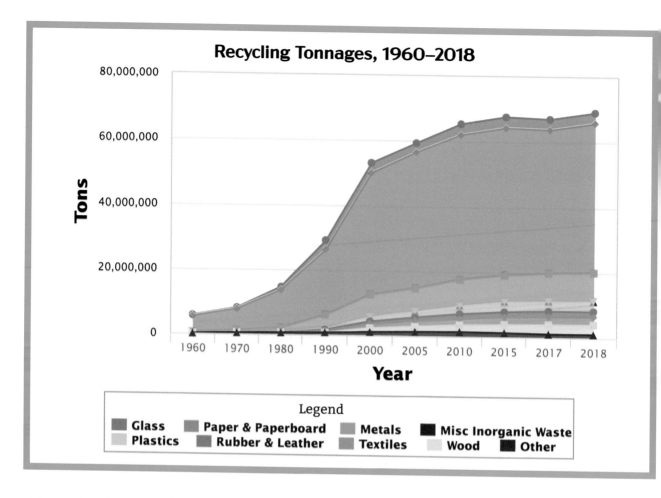

Recycling Tonnages, 1960–2018

Legend: Glass, Paper & Paperboard, Metals, Misc Inorganic Waste, Plastics, Rubber & Leather, Textiles, Wood, Other

Most single-use plastics are made from thermoplastic material. This kind of plastic can be recycled. But some of these items are not accepted in recycling programs. Straws, water bottle caps, and plastic shopping bags cause problems for recycling centers. Some are too small to be sorted. Others can jam the machines that process recycling.

Many grocery stores recycle plastic bags. They will even take clean single-use sandwich bags. But America may be making more single-use plastic than it can recycle.

There was a time when the US sent all the country's recyclable plastic to China. Unfortunately, a big percentage of that just ended up in Chinese landfills. In 2018, China decided it was time to solve its own waste problem. The country stopped accepting US plastic waste. While some plastic waste is still shipped to a few smaller countries, most of it stays in the country. This has created a new challenge.

Some cities do not always have the money for recycling programs. It is often cheaper to send things to the landfill. Also, some items like paper and certain plastic can only be recycled a few times. They become trash over time anyway. Cities often do not focus time and money on these special items.

The Yangtze River in China is the country's largest river. It is also one of the most polluted rivers in the world.

When recycling is done right, it can have amazing results. Americans use around 500 billion single-serve plastic water bottles per year. About 80 percent of them get thrown away. But they can be recycled into new bottles.

They can also be used to make new things. Recycled plastic lumber (RPL) is made from recycled bottles. Builders use it for decks and playgrounds. It lasts much longer than regular wood. Bottles can also be turned into a material used in clothing and shoes. Fourteen bottles can make filling for

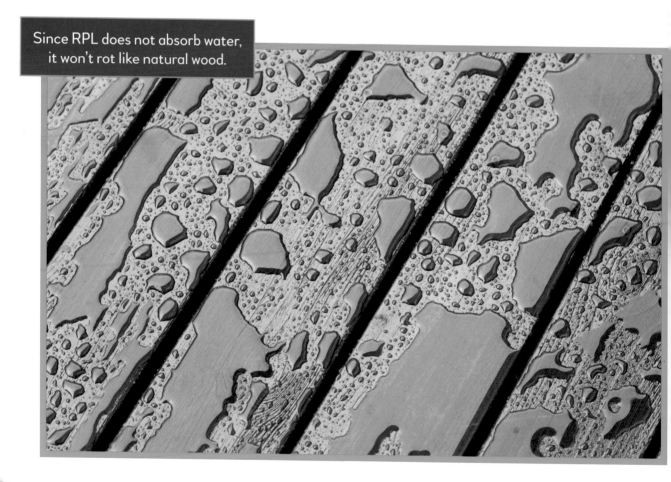

Since RPL does not absorb water, it won't rot like natural wood.

THIS BAG IS MADE FROM RECYCLED PLASTIC BOTTLES AND COTTON

one ski jacket. And 114 bottles can make the warm lining of a sleeping bag. They can even be used to make carpet. The caps from single-use water bottles can be made into car batteries, brooms, rope, yarn, and reusable shopping bags.

US shoppers use 100 billion plastic bags each year. They are expensive to recycle. They take many years to break down in a landfill. They slowly leak harmful toxins into the earth. These bags can be recycled to make new bags. But they can also be recycled into outdoor furniture, decks, and fences.

Many states don't allow metal in landfills. A single soda can take 100 years to break down. But it can be recycled or reused many times. Metal cans and even baking foil can be turned into steel beams and other building materials. Recycled cans are also used to make car and bike parts and appliances.

Glass can have a new use as **fiberglass** insulation. Recycled glass can be helpful as parts in water filtration devices. It can also be used to pave roads.

Tires are made up of natural rubber and several human-made ingredients. About 11 percent of tires end up in a landfill. They could be there for hundreds of years. And they take up a lot of space! But many more find a new life.

The Gift of Thrift

One of the biggest shopping trends of the 2020s is thrifting. Vintage styles have become fashionable. Thrift stores are the perfect place to shop those looks. Thrifting is a way to keep clothing and other items from being thrown away. And in the age of the internet, vintage fans can shop online. Sites such as Goodfair are online thrift stores that repurpose used clothing and sell it at reduced prices. Goodfair works with in-person thrift stores to "rescue" stock they cannot sell. Workers wash and prep items and send them to people in mystery batches. Goodfair's motto is "No New Things." They are doing their part to keep clothes out of landfills one T-shirt at a time.

Old tires can be used to make asphalt for roads. Running tracks are made of old tires. They can also be made into insulation. Whole tires can become swings and other playground equipment. Shredded tires keep kids safe while they play. Some people even use tires to build their homes.

Some things can be reused or **upcycled**. Furniture can be made from old wood. Old clothes are restyled or used to make new pieces. And some items can be donated and used again by others. You never know what treasures you might find in a thrift store!

CHAPTER 3

NEW IDEAS FOR OLD PROBLEMS

Waste is as old as humankind. People have been finding ways to deal with their trash for thousands of years. The first known public trash system was in ancient Greece. They used technology to dispose of it effectively. Technology is any method or system that solves a problem using scientific knowledge.

The ancient Greeks created a set of rules for how to manage their waste. Workers dug holes at least a mile outside the city to dump trash. It was also illegal for people to throw trash on the streets. The Greeks knew that having waste pile up near their homes was unhealthy. So they created a way to solve the problem. More than 2,000 years later, people are still inventing ways to deal with waste.

After his 2010 dive, Boyan Slat began to research garbage patches. He was just 18 when he invented a way to use the ocean's current to trap trash. Slat founded Ocean Cleanup in 2013. The company placed its first device in the Pacific Ocean in 2018. The floating system includes a large U-shaped barrier. It moves slowly through the water. It traps huge items, such as old fishing nets. But it also picks up and traps tiny microplastics.

The U-shaped barrier on Ocean Cleanup's floating system is 1,968.5 feet (600 meters) long.

Boyan Slat hopes to remove larger pieces of plastic from the ocean before they have a chance to degrade into harmful microplastics.

Slat's system collects waste. Then, large nets pull it out of the water. Ocean Cleanup works with companies. Together, they recycle the waste or make it into new things. The first product made from the trash they collected was designer sunglasses. They cost $199. This is enough to clean up another 24 football fields of ocean trash. The company uses 100 percent of the money from the glasses to fund future cleanups. And the sunglasses are also fully recyclable.

Ocean Cleanup has three trash-collecting devices in the Pacific Ocean so far. Their plan is to launch 60 more over the next several years. By 2040, they hope to have removed 90 percent of the garbage from the world's oceans. This waste could be used to make more than just sunglasses.

When large companies choose to make greener choices, they make a big impact. Volvo, a car company, has started replacing its leather seats with a product called Nordico. It is made from recycled plastic bottles, recycled cork, and other natural products. Other carmakers are following Volvo's lead.

Some experts say existing ways to clean the ocean, including Ocean Cleanup, are not effective. They create pollution and can disrupt sea creatures. Do you think it is better to try to solve one problem with the potential of creating another, or do nothing at all?

BMW is another car company. They plan to use less plastic altogether. BMW began making parts from plastic-free and **vegan** materials. BMW also joined forces with a company called Natural Fiber Welding. This company makes a product called Mirum. Mirum is made entirely out of plant matter. It can be used to make a leather-like replacement for car interiors. It is also used to make shoes and bags.

Natural Fiber Welding also makes a product called Clarus. It uses plant matter and recycled textiles. Clarus can be used to replace some fabrics that are used for clothing and shoes. Mirum and Clarus can be recycled again and again.

Extended Producer Responsibility

In 2021, Maine became the first US state to require product manufacturers to take responsibility for recycling their plastics and packaging materials. This means big companies have to pay for the cost of recycling the boxes, bags, and wrappings that contain their products. Other states are considering similar laws. Such laws are important steps in solving the country's trash problem. If manufacturers are responsible for the entire life of their product packaging, they are more likely to use packaging that costs less to recycle or can be used to make new product packaging.

Natural Fiber Welding is a circular company. When one of their products has been worn out, it can be returned and recycled. Most companies and manufacturers are not circular. When a person buys a product, they have to figure out what to do with it when it breaks or wears out. But a circular company takes responsibility for a product for its entire existence. There would be less waste in the world if more companies followed this model.

Most athletic shoes are made of fabric, rubber, and various plastics. People usually throw their old sneakers away when they wear out. Around 300 million pairs are thrown away every year. It can take up to 40 years for one pair to break down in a landfill. Nike and adidas are two of the top brands hoping to change this.

Adidas partnered with a company called Parley for the Oceans in 2015. Their adidas x Parley collection is shoes made from ocean plastic. Adidas made more than 30 million pairs of sneakers from recycled plastic in 2020.

Nike makes its leather, rubber, and nylon from recycled materials. In 2018, Nike was recognized for using more recycled polyester than anyone else in the textile industry. They turned 6.4 billion plastic water bottles into polyester between 2010 and 2018. In 2020, they launched a campaign called Move to Zero. The company hopes to keep 99 percent of all shoe manufacturing waste out of landfills. Circular manufacturing is another step. Nike's Reuse-a-Shoe and Nike Grind programs turn old shoes into new shoes, playgrounds, and athletic courts.

Nike's Reuse-a-Shoe program has collected 28 million shoes to recycle since 1990.

Making new buildings and tearing down old ones creates a lot of waste. In 2018, about 145 million tons (131.5 metric tons) of construction waste filled US landfills. But recycling is also part of the waste stream. Even though a lot of construction waste ends up in a landfill, about 76 percent of it is reused or recycled.

Many items used in the construction industry are already recyclable. Steel, asphalt, and wood have been used to build things for hundreds of years. These products can be reused or turned into new materials. Many cities have construction recycling centers where builders can take unused materials.

New products such as RPL are helping builders even more. RPL is made from milk jugs, water bottles, and some plastic shopping bags. RPL is mostly used for outdoor building. Decks, fences, and benches are examples. It lasts much longer than wood. RPL does not need to be painted. It does not rot or crack. It is easy to clean. Best of all, it does not absorb mold and other bacteria.

Some sustainable, longer-lasting products are often more expensive. Do you think that might stop some people from trying them?

Yellowstone National Park chose RPL for this viewing area of Old Faithful, which shoots water into the air anywhere from every 44 minutes to 2 hours. RPL is waterproof, weather-resistant, and long-lasting.

Aluminum

The aluminum icon means the object is made from recyclable aluminum.

The Green Dot

This symbol lets us know the producer supports recycling programs.

Mobius Loop

This universally recognized logo means an item is capable of being recycled.

Glass

This mark reminds us to dispose of glass bottles and jars in a bottle bank or a glass household recycling collection.

Waste Electricals

From home appliances to mobile phones, items with this symbol can be recycled.

Compostable

The Biodegradable Products Institute created this logo to help consumers know what items are compostable.

Changing the way companies make things is a huge first step. These changes can help reduce waste. But long-lasting impacts can only happen if people are willing to change too. Making waste is easy. Throwing items in the trash does not take much thought. Recycling takes more time and effort. It can take some planning. It can be a little gross. But hopefully it will pay off in the end.

But recycling alone is not the solution to America's waste problem. In order to waste less plastic, Americans must use less plastic. The US recycling system is limited. Some scientists think we are making more single-use items than we can ever recycle. Even if we can deal with some of it, there is still waste that rots in the landfill. It is time to rethink the items we choose in the first place.

Buying food packaged in glass instead of plastic can help. So can buying fresh food instead of pre-packaged or processed items. Some companies use biodegradable packaging. It is impossible to avoid using plastic all together. But it is important for families to do their research. Be aware of what goes into the things you use each day. When customers are willing to pay for eco-friendly things, companies listen.

What was the last packaged food you bought or ate? How could its packaging be made more eco-friendly?

Although they cost a bit more at first, reusable items last much longer. Over time, their value will outweigh their cost. Lunch bags, water bottles, and reuseable shopping bags are examples. You can use them over and over again. A good reusable item will last a long time.

Straws are another reusable option. Many cities in America have gotten rid of plastic straws completely. Metal straws can be used instead. Some companies provide a carrying case with multiple straws inside. You can bring them wherever you go. Glass straws are a good option for home use. They come in pretty colors too!

Some states have banned plastic shopping bags. And there are many other options for running errands. Reusable bags come in many shapes and sizes. They are made of many different materials. Bright colors or designs make them fun to collect and show off. Some stores offer a discount to shoppers who bring their own bags. Others print their own logos on the bags. It's a great form of free advertising.

What reusable items does your family use every day?
What single-use items could you swap for reusable ones?

The average person uses 156 plastic water bottles per year. One reusable water bottle would keep these from ending up in a landfill.

Moving from plastic bottles to reusable ones will probably have the biggest impact. People in the US open approximately 1,000 plastic water bottles per second. Using refillable bottles could keep billions of plastic bottles out of America's landfills.

Families who commit to recycling can help change the future and make Earth a healthier place to live.

The United States has been recycling since the 1960s. Cities such as San Francisco have shown the rest of the country what can happen when recycling is done well. They have a goal of zero waste. It has led to 80 percent less trash being dumped in the area's landfills. But recycling alone cannot bring about zero waste across the country.

Manufacturers are beginning to change the way they make the things they sell. Laws about what can be thrown away are pushing people to think about what they buy. Technology continues to help us clean up decades of waste. It also continues to help reduce the amount of waste we make.

America has a trash problem for sure. Landfills are overflowing. Plastic is taking over the ocean. Families throw away items that could be recycled. But there are ways to help. And if every individual does their part, it might be possible to get rid of landfills and plastic bottles completely.

Activity 1:

Create something new from something old. Use too-small or old clothes to design a new article of clothing, or make a work of art from broken, used, or discarded items in your home. Put it on display!

MATERIALS:

- old clothes, broken items, or plastic jugs, cans, and so on from the recycling bin
- scissors
- glue
- other items such as glitter, buttons, or ribbon to add finishing touches to your creation

PROCEDURE

Use the internet to search for the perfect project for you. You could make an herb garden from soup cans, a decorative holiday village from toilet paper and paper towel rolls, or a comfy pillow from too-small t-shirts. The possibilities are endless!

Activity 2:

Plan a cleanup day at a local park, river, stream, beach, or someplace else. Get in touch with your local recycling center ahead of time so they can help you sort everything the right way to make the biggest impact.

MATERIALS:

- poster board and markers
- trash bags
- disposable gloves

PROCEDURE:

1. Pick an area to clean up. It could be a neighborhood park or a section of a stream or river.

2. Work with your teacher to decide on a good day and time. Your teacher can help you contact community leaders if necessary.

3. Make posters to advertise your event. Include the location, the start time, and how long the cleanup will last.

4. Pick up trash!

GLOSSARY

CARBON MONOXIDE (KAR-buhn muh-NOKS-eyed): a harmful gas made by burning plastic and certain chemicals

COMPOSTING (KOM-pose-ting): mixing food and yard waste together with soil to create a natural fertilizer called humus

CONTAMINATED (con-TAM-uh-nay-tuhd): dirty or poisoned

DECOMPOSE (de-kom-POSE): to rot

FIBERGLASS (FY-buhr-glass): a lightweight material made from thin threads of glass

GARBAGE PATCH (GAR-buhj PATCH): a large area of trash in the ocean created by the current

LEACH (LEECH): the process that occurs when a solid breaks down into a liquid form and runs into soil

OBSOLESCENCE (ob-suh-LESS-uhns): the process of going out of date or becoming useless

POLLUTE (pol-OOT): to make dirty or unsafe

UPCYCLED (UP-sigh-kuhld): the process of turning something old into a new product

VEGAN (VEE-guhn): a food or item that does not contain anything made from animals or animal products

FOR MORE INFORMATION

BOOKS

Carlton, Victoria. *The Plastic Problem: 60 Small Ways to Reduce Waste*. Oakland, CA: Lonely Planet Kids, 2020.

Gogerly, Liz. *Go Green!* Minneapolis, MN: Free Spirit Publishing Inc., 2019.

Romer, Jenny. *Can I Recycle This?: A Guide to Better Recycling and How to Reduce Single-Use Plastics*. New York, NY: Penguin Books, 2021.

WEBSITES

Kids Guide to Recycling
https://www.reusethisbag.com/articles/kids-guide-to-recycling
Learn even more about the importance of recycling and how to leave the planet a better place.

Recycle
https://kids.niehs.nih.gov/topics/reduce/recycle/index.htm
Find out what can and can't be recycled. You might be surprised!

Recycling
https://www.ducksters.com/science/environment/recycling_for_kids.php
How does recycling work? This site breaks it down into simple steps.

INDEX

ABOUT THE AUTHOR

Heather DiLorenzo Williams is a writer and educator with a passion for seeing readers of all ages connect with others through stories and personal experiences. She enjoys running, reading, and watching sports. Heather lives in North Carolina with her husband and two children.